Judith Turner
Photographs Five Architects

Judith Turner
Photographs Five Architects

Introduction by John Hejduk

The highest problem of any art is to cause by
appearance the illusion of a higher reality.
Goethe

Contents

Introduction

The Flatness of Depth

Part I

I will have to approach some of the issues confronted in Judith Turner's volume of photographs of architecture, or more specifically her photographs of the parts and fragments of architecture, in an elliptical way.

I must lay out in some vague yet apparently understandable way the process that "architecture" or the making of architecture goes through in order to peripherally touch the edges of what lies on the surface of Judith Turner's photographs. I hope that I can also get at what lies at the heart of their existence – at their depths, their very fabrications.

I come to this complex issue of photography and architecture as an architect and therefore not entirely as a stranger. The problems of conception, image, representation, and realization are haunting obsessions to my mind's eye. The many masks of apparent reality have made me wonder, speculate, and ponder about the revealed and the unrevealed.

I can conceive of (imagine in my mind) a jug, an apple, a table, and within my mind put them into some compositional relationship.

I can then take these imagined objects (jug, apple, table) and draw them upon a two-dimensional surface (upon a piece of paper). That is, I can represent that which I imagined fixed in a frame. Drawn on a two-dimensional piece of paper what I had imagined is an illusion, yet it is also a realization, that is, the reality of a drawing on a sheet of paper. The above moves deal with conception, representation, and realization.

I can also conceive of fabricating a jug and table as I previously imagined them into so-called actual three-dimensional objects. And I am able to fabricate a representation of an apple or even search for a real apple that closely matches my imagined one and then use it in a three-dimensional jug-apple-table arrangement-composition.

Once the objects are selected and made, I can place all three three-dimensional objects in a three-dimensional relationship in a three-dimensional space – that is, in a so-called actual or real space.

I can then make a film with the camera moving 360 degrees around the recently constructed fabrication. I can even film the still life with changing light (natural?) from dawn to darkness, or I can fabricate the light sources.

I have often thought that when we actually move physically in space our mind takes a secondary position to our body's tactile sensations. When we physically stop moving and become fixed, our mind takes over the primary position. How often while walking when deep in thought do we suddenly realize that we have no recollection of having walked from point A to point B. When our mind is working intensively, our body, for all intents and purposes, seems to be fixed and might as well not be in motion.

I can also take still photographs of the jug-apple-table. That is, in effect, a fixed photograph of a representation of a fabrication.

Actual objects (idea-compositional elements) remain fixed, yet the quality of light on objects and the observer of objects can change.

The photograph is a fixed recording. Film movement, the tracking of a fixed object from various points of view, the moving of the cinema camera and the motion picture are acutely different in concept from the singular fixed photograph.

I can also contemplate the object moving in relationship to a fixed observer as well as the object fixed to a moving observer.

These notes have to do with so-called naturalistic objects such as the jug-apple-table, which is under observation.

I can conceive of a series of non-objective representations – for instance, a black vertical line crossing a black horizontal line, off center upon a white square field. I can conceive of a flat non-objective painting where the image is flat, followed by the representation of the flat painting re-presented flat, and the realization of the flat painting where the reality is flat. I could also take a photograph (same size) of the flat, non-objective painting. For the moment, I will leave the reader some time to think about this proposition.

Some questions come up: What is the reality of architecture? What are architectural representations of reality? Is its (architecture) realization absolutely necessary?

The re-presentation of an actuality is most important: how the so-called reality can, in fact, represent itself in architecture – as, perhaps, in a non-objective Mondrian painting.

I believe that full comprehension of an object involves the least physical movement of the observer. I can speculate that painting is fixed, sculpture is fixed, and architecture is fixed.

In a Mondrian painting, reality is conceived, reality is represented, reality is realized. All are one and the same thing.

Architecture must of necessity rely on the least fixed set of circumstances. It must also put reality into a frame. The so-called reality is transformed.

In cinema, although a "real thing" is filmed, it goes through a transformation. First, the real image is shot, bringing it to the surface of the film. Next, the image on film is projected upon a two-dimensional screen-frame, and then images are put into motion. Film, even when in motion, is never full-depth. At most, it is ¾-depth, and when the film is stopped suddenly it becomes totally flat as in a still photograph.

Part II

There are many kinds of architectural realities and interpretations of those realities, which include the major issue of representation or re-presentation. Whatever the medium used – be it a pencil sketch on paper, a small-scale model, the building itself, a sketch of the built building, a model of the built building, a film of the built building, or a photograph of the above realities – a process is taking place. Some sort of distortion is occurring, a distortion that has to do with intuition as primal yearning, which, in turn, has something to do with the interpretation and reinterpretation of space and all the mysteries the word space encompasses, including its spirit.

Whatever the initial catalyst is, let us assume that an architect has an architectural image inside his mind's eye. The initial image is like a single still-frame, because I do not believe that at first any architect has a total image of an entire architecture simultaneously – to my experience or knowledge, it doesn't work that way. There may be a series of images one after the other over a period of time, but that period of time, no matter how small, is a necessary ingredient for the evolution toward a totality. It must be understood that so-called total architecture is ultimately made up of parts and fragments and fabrications. Put in another way, when we look at a painting, we see the total image at once. Of course, after the initial viewing of the presented image, our mind, through our eyes, can have the pleasure of rummaging through the painting, revealing all its intended subtleties and nuances and some of its mysteries. We are able to study it. But the whole so-called real image we can see immediately. To some degree, the same can be said of sculpture, although the three-dimensionality of sculpture makes this more complicated. However, except for the kind of sculpture that tends or pretends toward the architecture of no program, we, as observers, tend to hover over or encompass sculpture.

Architecture can be observed both from a distance and internally (close-up); we can become internally ingested by it, become part of its interior. Instead of just being an outside observer or an outside spectator, we can become part of its very interior organism. We become physical-organic participators; we become enclosed. Architecture is the only art form that affords us the opportunity of being voyeurs who watch the outside from the outside and also of being interior watchers. We can also observe the inside from the outside, the outside from the inside, and the inside from the inside. It is all made up of a series of outside fragments and inside fragments.

We are always faced with the illusion of depth-realities. I would like to take each of the processes of architectural evolution and speak of the depth-realities of images, conceptions, apparent realization, and the manner of presentation and representation and translation.

The architect can make a number of representations on a blank, two-dimensional sheet of paper. He is able to draw images of ideas upon its surface. In drawing plans, elevations, or sections, he is basically making notations that run parallel to the paper's surface. He is also able to make isometrics, axonometrics, and perspectives into the surface, each one giving a different depth connotation ranging from the shallowness of an isometric to the extended deepness of a perspective. All are specifically real (pencil on paper), all are representations of proposed comings, and all are illusions regarding space and depth. Although the perspective is the most heightened illusion – whereas the representation of a plan may be considered the closest to reality – if we consider it as substantively notational, the so-called reality of built architecture can only come into being through a notational system. In any case, drawing on a piece of paper is an architectural reality.

The next step is the possibility of making a scale model of the intended future realization. By and large, the scale model is usually at a reduced scale in three dimensions: we are much larger than it, we hover about it and walk around it, we hold it in our hands, etc. The model has been made by putting together a series of two-dimensional coordinates, so that it too is illusionary, a fabrication. It too is an architectural reality somehow closer to the isometric and axonometric than to perspective reality on paper. Full-scale models of fragmentations of buildings can be made, yet they seem removed as they are.

The architecture is then built. It too is a realization based on another reality, and a number of interesting conditions emerge regarding the hypothetical observer. From a far distance, the observer can see the built architecture as an object similar to the model, although he is not able to see the so-called totality unless he sets himself into motion to investigate it from many points of view in the three-dimensional reality.

After the work of architecture has been built into the real world, further re-presentations are possible. We can make sketches of the existing structure; we can make a film of the existing structure; and we can make photographs of the built structure. Of course, throughout history architecture was the subject of travel sketches. Ingres, Dürer, Le Corbusier, and others practiced their hand about this subject as information. It does seem to me that to look upon architecture built through drawn information is proper. However, re-drawing it after building somehow seems less satisfactory, whereas the initial drawings appear fresher. To make a model of the built object seems more substantive and, in a strange way, is very like the pre-built model of the architecture. This, then, leaves us with two other modes of re-presentation – film and still photography. But before we take a look at these two later conditions, let's go back to our hypothetical observer. As the hypothetical observer approaches the architecture, the building simply becomes larger, and the observer sees more and more detail. His position is changed from that of hoverer over the object to one of the object hovering over the observer. It is as if the piece of architecture has swallowed up the hypothetical observer, as if he has become part of its internal gestation system. Of course, he can be expelled through the membrane to reverse his former trek at any time. This set-up is unique to architecture.

Now, our hypothetical observer can repeat the same journey two more times – with a cinema camera in his hand taking moving pictures and once with a camera in his hand taking fixed pictures. In both cases, the observed images have been framed. The film is developed and projected on a screen, and our observer is seated in a darkened room. He is fixed while he sees a moving film upon a fixed screen. The moving film, as I stated previously, is in appearance never full-depth, but approximately ¾-depth.

Now, perhaps the most profound confrontation of all takes place – the fixed observer looking at a photograph, a single photograph, a single, still, fixed photograph, a fixed observer seeing a fixed photograph, a most reduced confrontation. The mind of the observer is heightened to an extreme, exorcising out from a single fixed photographic image all its possible sensations and meanings – a fragment of time suspended, a recapturing of the very image that has been photographed.

Which brings me to the subject at hand: Judith Turner's photographs of architecture.

Part III

At first appearances, the subject of Judith Turner's photographs is architecture, although the meaning of the photographs (outside of their visual beauty and superb compositional precision) has to do with the degree of abstraction. To what extent does the subject matter (architecture) hold to its own inner essence? What kind of dialogue is going on between the observer (Judith Turner) and the observed (architecture)? Is it possible to capture the very essence of a subject in a single still photograph? Perhaps an additional inquiry could be, why does Judith Turner focus on the fragments (details) of architecture? This leads us to the overwhelming question, when the subject matter is in fact abstract to begin with, does it survive further abstraction, or does a profound transformation take place?

To begin with the general questions, Judith Turner does in fact follow the path of the discussion in Parts I and II of this introduction. She understands that it is impossible to see architecture in its full complexity at once. Architecture *is* made up of details, fragments, fabrications. And the very idea behind it can be captured in a fragment, in a detail. And architecture is made up of two dimensions. Judith Turner does believe that the very essence of the spirit of an architecture can be captured in a single still photograph. She also knows that there is a precarious balance between the re-presentation of the subject and its realities. In some cases, the further abstraction is pushed; it de-materializes the very subject of its existence. The most profound architectures carry the same seed, the same essences, in whatever realities they are "re-presented" in.

Judith Turner is able to re-present the abstraction and the substantive materiality of the subject matter in a dialectic of her own vision of realities, her own vision of photography as a creative act. Hers is the creation of a single still photograph of haunting visual beauty.

Judith Turner is also making a critical commentary on that which she photographs. Her art has to do with fixed silences upon abstracted thoughts. She searches for an unforgettable moment, like it or not, and she reveals sparsities and densities – the basic substance of architecture.

She is in love with white, black, and gray and the way light softly washes surfaces in gentle ways. She informs opaque surfaces and translucent ones too. She is fascinated by the juxtaposition of the forms and shapes of architecture, the vocabulary of the elements of the elemental. She is obsessed by stairs, handrails, skylights, windows, columns and beams, the way things fit together, the way they argue. She wants her solitary viewer to know that architecture is abstract, is still-life. The materiality of glass, cement, plaster, steel, aluminum, wood, and galvanized metal is celebrated and honored through her photography.

In a curious way, she shows the differences in the architectures presented. She shows what each architect is really interested in through her silent witness – the photograph.

Judith Turner's vision is subtle, precise, impeccable, exacting, abstract, compositional, and quietly moving. She senses the materiality and the details. She knows space, and she is able to re-present it into something of her own, into another creative reality. Her photographs provoke thought in depth. She captures still moments. Judith Turner is an artist of rare creative sensibilities, and we are the recipients of her gifts.

John Hejduk, Dean
The Cooper Union
School of Architecture
March 1980

Charles Gwathmey and
Robert Siegel, Architects
Kislevitz Residence
West Hampton Beach
New York, 1976

Peter Eisenman, Architect
House VI, Frank Residence
Cornwall, Connecticut, 1976

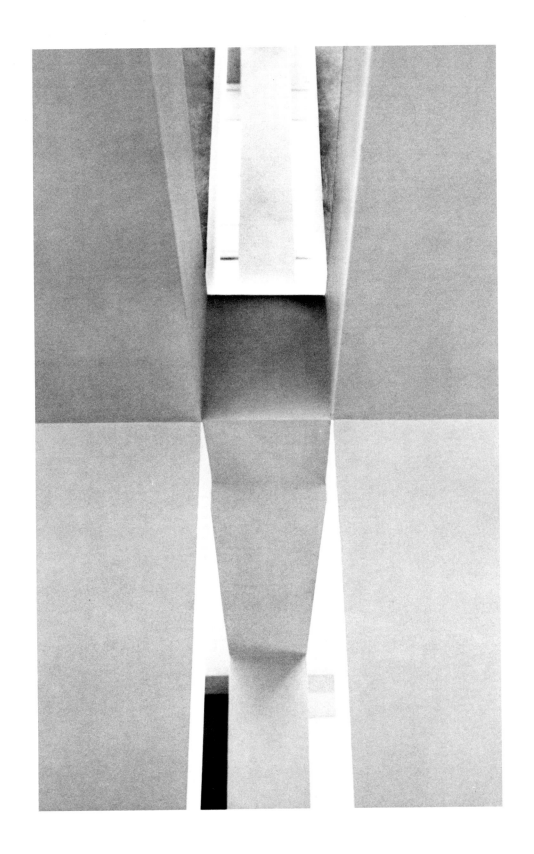

John Hejduk, Architect
Peter Bruder, Engineer
Ed Aviles, Associate Architect
The Cooper Union Renovation
New York, New York, 1974-75

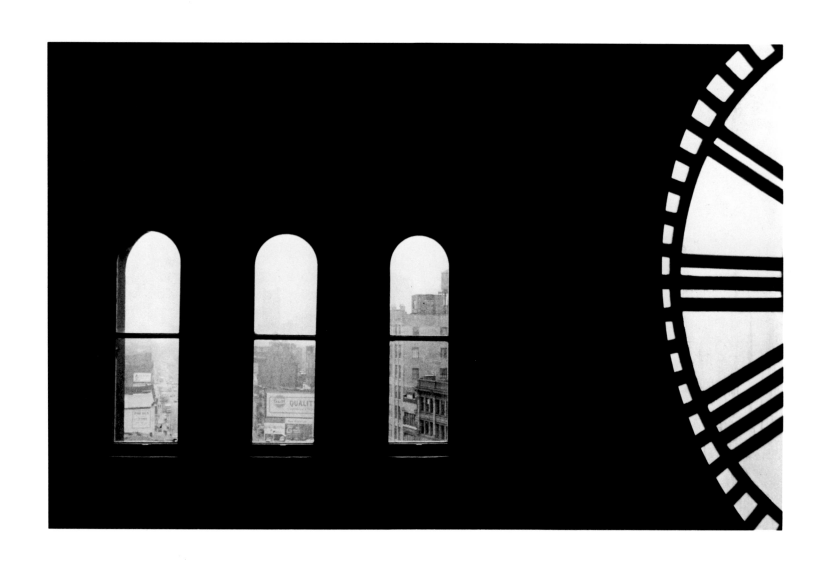

Michael Graves, Architect
Benacerraf House Addition
Princeton, New Jersey, 1969

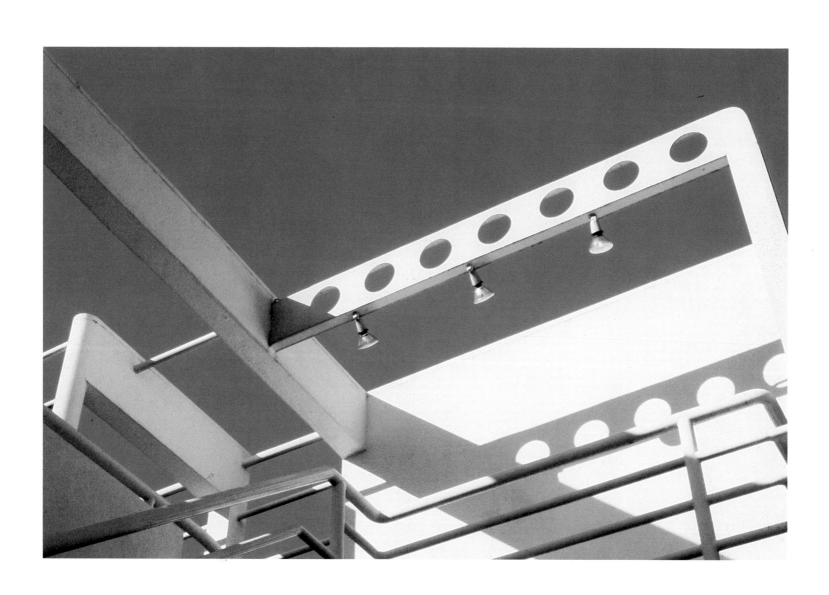

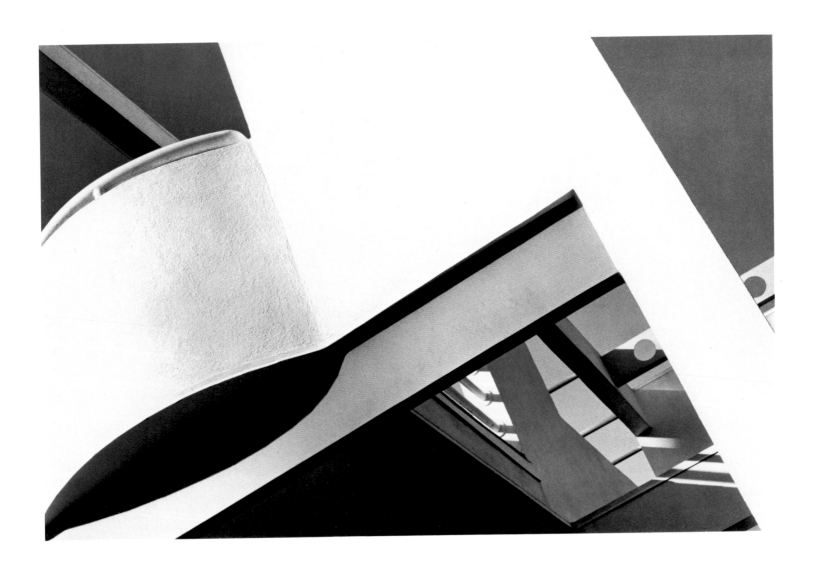

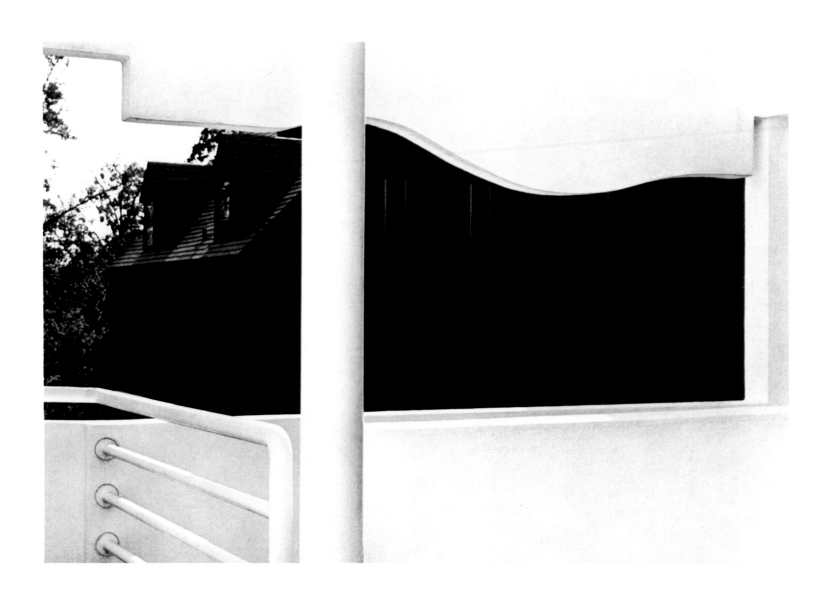

Richard Meier, Architect
Bronx Developmental Center
Bronx, New York, 1977